This book belongs to:

____

Made in United States
Orlando, FL
16 January 2024

42577444R00065